THE FLOW LANE

Creating Life One Thought at a Time

WRITTEN BY LYNN M ROBINSON

WITH KIM SMITH

An Unbelievable Freedom Book

*Going with the flow doesn't mean that
we don't know where we're going;
it means that we are open to multiple ways of getting there.
Going with the flow means that we are aware of an energy
that is larger than our small selves,
and we are open to working with it, not against it.*

MADISYN TAYLOR

*To all the souls out there who know deep
within that this is not all there is:*

May you find the strength within yourself to seek out the truth.

*May your search awaken your inspiration and set you on
a path to create a life beyond your wildest dreams.*

Table of Contents

Welcome from Kim

Greetings!

Thanks for reading *The Flow Lane: Creating Life One Thought at a Time*. It's the 5th Unbelievable Freedom Book in the format of a workbook-style Habit Guide, and this time, it's about using our thoughts to experience life in new and powerful ways. This is a topic that interests me greatly, so it will appear throughout the series. Above all, Unbelievable Freedom is a mindset and I want our readers to be empowered in that knowledge. I want you to believe that your mindset can always be sculpted to invite more freedom.

As for this author, I've known Lynn Robinson for several years, dating back to when we worked for the same hospital system. From the moment I met Lynn, I was drawn to her energy. Even though it sounds cliched, she has a captivating aura. Her energy is vibrant but gentle at the same time. She has a perpetual smile and twinkling eyes. Her positive outlook sparked my curiosity and I began following her social media accounts, including her virtual book club focused on books related to personal growth and spirituality.

Since we met, Lynn has gone on to become a holistic practitioner, offering Reiki and other energy work to humans and animals. She is a devoted student of the Law of Attraction, and she believes in creating a sense of flow by channeling positive thoughts in daily life. I couldn't wait to get her involved with Unbelievable Freedom Habit Guides, and I can't wait for you to read what she has in store in the pages ahead.

Enjoy Your Life,
Kim

Introduction

Each person begins in their own space, in their own time, and in their own way. All we have is now, today, so that's where we start.

My journey of spiritual awakening has been over the last five years. With this enlightenment, I see much clearer why I experienced the mountains and the valleys. I created them; all of them. The good and the "not so good" in my life. Taking full responsibility for my life wasn't easy. I would bring in the 'coincidences' and 'circumstances beyond my control' theories to shift off some of the weight. In the end, however, I "chose" to do, say or think it all and by choosing I created my outcome.

So what if we did choose to take control of our thinking? Would our lives drastically change? That's how it worked for me.

My intent with writing this workbook is to provide you with new thought patterns and give you exercises to help you practice implementing these thought patterns into your own life. The topics are ones that I have personally accepted into practice and I will share with you examples of how they have in turn changed me.

My wish is for you to start creating a life by intent and stop creating by default; a life where feeling good becomes addictive.

When we are in the flow of life things move easily, free of stress and tension. You can start right now creating your life in a more positive way, by stepping into The Flow Lane.

Start Saying Yes!

Were you shy as a child? I was. Debilitating shyness. That's how I would describe it. I could make new friends but it was not easy. This made my teenage years a challenge and as I matured into a young adult, it didn't get any easier. The next 20 years of my adult life was spent avoiding making eye contact. Smile at a stranger? No way! I will forever remember one time I was placing mail in a receptacle outside a store when a man came up next to me to mail his letters. He said hello. I couldn't look up, couldn't respond. I just high-tailed it out of there! It seems comical to me now and a little sad that I couldn't successfully interact with other humans.

Today, I speak in front of groups of people, physicians and CEOs alike, and can make new friends without even breaking a sweat. So what did I do? What was the turning point? I knew I wanted freedom. Freedom from this limitation. I wanted to experience LIFE! So here's the key . . . I started saying yes. Yes to my friends who asked me to do something I've never done. Yes to asking a stranger for help. Was it easy? No, it was a challenge every single time but with each attempt, I gained something . . . personal power. Retraining your brain for anything takes time and practice but it's so worth it.

I said yes to taking a vacation to Nashville with a beautiful soul I had met only 6 months earlier

I said yes to participating in not only one but TWO Tough Mudder Obstacle races in one year.

I said yes to hauling my horse hours away to a beach to ride him through the surf and sand.

I said yes when I was asked to write this book.

I don't think I was shy as a child, but I
didn't have many friends, until 8th grade. That was pivotal for me,
setting me up to be the friendly, outgoing person in high school.

There is no more fear. There is only excitement. I'm more excited about what the next new experience is going to bring to my life than of any fear of failure. The worst that has ever happened to me by saying yes is that I found out I most likely will not do something again.

Are you blocking the experience of something wonderful in your life because of a limiting belief? What can you start saying yes to today? Jot them down. You can start small but start by saying YES!

Yes! to going hiking by myself (once I'm strong enough).

Yes! to projects around the house. I am worth it. I can learn new things, like painting, fixing seams in walls + more.

Yes! to shades in our bedroom.

The Empty Drawer

Most of us walk around saying things like "There are no decent men out there" or "I'm never going to find a good woman". When someone asks us what is it that we are looking for in a partner, we actually look at them with a blank stare and can't seem to come up with a good answer. Herein lies the problem. Have you ever sat down and actually put some thought into what you consider a good match for you? I never had. I mean, isn't it all by chance that we will meet our partner anyway? I'm here to tell you that if vague is what you put out there, vague is what you're going to get.

Start making a list of attributes, activities, and future goals that you want your partner to have for the relationship. When I say make a list, I want you to be SPECIFIC! Tall, funny, dresses nice, non-smoker, sexy grin, loves the outdoors, athletic, holds your hand, kisses you in public, loves animals, etc. Ok, so these may be some things on my list but you are getting the idea of how to start.

You've made your list. Now what? We make room for that person in our life. Yes, I have just upped the game. We need to start believing that our partner is on his or her way so we need to get ready. So empty out one dresser drawer, leave one coat hook empty, leave out two coffee mugs by the coffee maker, and this one is going to hurt, but make some room in your closet. Donate to Goodwill, put some of your clothes in storage, whichever way is fine. No one is going to question your sanity. No one but you needs to know. You are now on a mission. You have put down every detail of what you want in a partner AND you have made room for this person in your life.

Does this really work? I have attracted my last two relationships by this tried and true method. What I realized from the first one is that I was not specific enough. So my list expanded, I made room in my life, and the next one arrived. Here is the best part. Once you see this in action, you will start believing and once you start believing, you start to trust. You trust that you are deserving to have a partner that matches your specific wants. You trust that you will rendezvous with this person in the very near future.

After my last relationship ended, I decided to 'up' my game even further. I thought wouldn't it be fun to be able to 'text' my future husband as if he already existed. So I decided to dig out my old Tracfone, edited the contact name to 'Hubby' and started sending texts to it. Texts that I would send to my husband such as 'I love you', 'I'm so glad you are in my life', 'I'm on my way home soon', 'Good night', 'good morning', etc. I was loving this new exercise and having fun at the same time! I said to myself, I won't be surprised when one day that number calls me and it's my husband. That was a Friday night.

Three days later, my phone rang. The caller ID showed . . . "Hubby". The date was 11/11, a Monday morning. The number 3 in itself is a powerful number in the Universe and the use of 11/11 was also the universe using numerology as a clear sign. The caller was not my 'husband' unfortunately as the Tracfone company had reassigned my number due to it not being used for a certain period of time. But this was a powerful response from the universe saying to me, 'So you want to play? Let's play".

Make your list. Make room. Believe.

The Secret Revealed

The truth is that we attract what we think about. The Law of Attraction is a Universal Law just like the Law of Gravity. If we can believe in Karma, then we already believe that there is some greater universal force at work. Attraction in this sense means the process of "attracting" things into our lives by way of our thinking. Sounds a bit like magic?

The Law of Attraction says: That which is like unto itself, is drawn.

When you wake up in the morning feeling unhappy, and then throughout the day things get worse and worse, then at the end of the day you say, "I shouldn't have gotten out of bed". You also see this evidenced with a person who only speaks of illness has illness; and one who only speaks of prosperity has prosperity.

Because the Law of Attraction is responding to the thoughts that you hold at all times, it is accurate to say that you are creating your own reality. Since it is not possible to monitor our every thought, we need to start by slowly re-programming our mind to think more GOOD thoughts. I have found the best method that worked for me in the beginning was redirection. When I was experiencing a negative thought or feeling, I would instantly think of something that makes me happy.

 This process takes time. So do not get discouraged if it takes you awhile to get this into a habit. You didn't learn to walk in one day, but you did eventually not only walk but learn to run. Start by making a list of things that make you happy and this will be your go-to list of "distractions". Puppies, fuzzy blankets, hot coffee, your child's smile, once you start your list you'll find that you have lots of things that instantly put a smile on your face.

Now at first, you will redirect but that negative thought may quickly return. I promise you that the more you keep redirecting, the less negative thoughts will come and the less you will need to use this exercise. Because guess what you started? You have started a steady flow of positive thoughts which the Universe is responding to. This will become your new normal! You are creating your own Flow Lane!

Since understanding this Law, I have drastically changed my life. For example, whenever a new bill comes in the mail that I didn't anticipate, I tell myself that "there is always an abundance of money" and I give it no more thought. I have done this so often that it is almost instantaneous those words come into my mind. I give that bill no power over me. I don't let it consume any of my time worrying over how I'm going to pay it.

This next part I'm going to say may be a bit startling to some of you so hold on, but I have not balanced my checkbook in over 5 years. Take a breath. I know I just freaked some of you out. That is how far I have come in not letting money control me. I always EXPECT there to be money in my checking account when it's time to pay my bills, and there always is. Money will flow to you from many different sources and in ways that you never anticipated. When you think about abundance, abundance will come to you.

The secret is knowing how powerful your thoughts are.

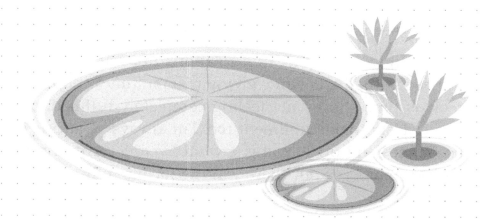

What You *(really)* Want, Wants You!

We have all looked at something and thought to ourselves that 'I want that'. Maybe even looked at a person that we thought was attractive and thought 'I want that person for a partner!' Fast forward and one day you think back and say to yourself "thank goodness that never came true!" What we have now in our life is so much better.

Sometimes we need to stop and think when we find ourselves wanting something and consider if we want what it is or do we want what it represents. In other words, do you want that big house on the hill or do you *really* want a home where you feel safe, secure and loved?

This is how we fine-tune what we want in our lives. Taking the time to actually contemplate on why we are attracted to certain things will reveal mountains of information about ourselves.

What you *really* want, wants you. This relates to your inner being, the one that knows what is for your highest and best; the part of you that really wants a deep connection with a partner; the part of you that really wants a job that lets your creativity flow through. Feel your way through to what you really want. Your inner guidance is always there and always uses your emotions to help you line up with what you *really* want. If what you are thinking of does not fill you with happiness, then it's not for you. Accept that. Move on.

Never, never settle for less than feeling good. Sometimes life will give us stepping blocks to move towards what we really want and that's ok. Sometimes we fine-tune as we experience what we don't want. Just don't stay there. Use the contrast of different situations to let you know what you DON'T want and thus making it clear what you DO want. Life causes us to expand. The universe will continually send us new things to match our expansion.

For me, I just can't stay in a relationship that isn't growing with me. Trust me, I've tried 'hanging on' and 'giving it some time' and in the end, all I've done is let precious time slip by not feeling completely fulfilled, and honestly, I've kept my partner from their fulfillment too. I'm always so appreciative of these opportunities. What I end up learning is what I *really* want in a relationship. This person, this best match, is out there waiting for me to line up with him. He will be what I really want.

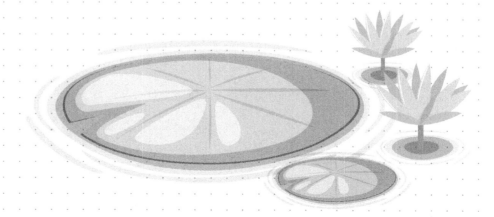

No more wasting time with vagueness! Can you think of areas in your life where you have been less than honest with yourself in what you want? Areas where you have not truly defined what it is that you want? Start sprinkling on some specificity in different aspects of your life and see what starts showing up!

Remember if it doesn't make you feel fabulous; don't do it, don't buy it, don't wear it, don't eat it, don't keep it.

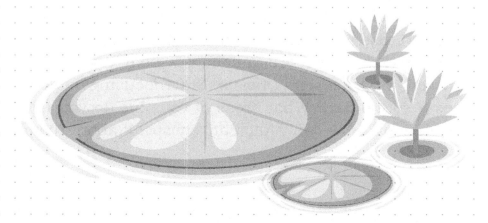

Stop It!

Amy Jo Ellis is a name in the energy healing community and I was first told about her by a mutual friend. After following Amy Jo for a few months, I found that she did a YouTube series on becoming aware of our internal dialogues. Now mind you, I have been working on my own internal dialogue for a few years at this point but I know that there are always new aspects to learn so I instantly signed up for her 14-day challenge called 'Stop It!' and realized that I can be doing better in many more areas.

What has always amazed me is how easy it is for us as humans to make an impotent statement of observation otherwise known as "a complaint". Take a look at what it is that you would rather have. Amy Jo suggests changing the habit of complaining to the habit of creative speech. This is the part that I have found challenging, yet fun is trying to find a vocabulary that feels good when I say it!

Let's try some phrases just so you can see how they "feel" as you say them.

"I never have any time to read a book!"

"If I spend less time each day watching puppies do tricks online, I can start reading that book I've been wanting to."

"I hate my job!"

"Sometimes I feel under-appreciated in my job, but it does provide the money I need to support my family."

"That person is 'dying' of cancer."

"That person is 'living' with cancer."

Can you feel the difference in those statements? We do not realize how the harsh words we use affect our nervous system. Just by doing the exercise above, you should feel the difference in how your body reacts to your words. So, go easy on yourself. Stop the self-criticism. Start focusing on your internal dialogue. What does it sound like? What areas of your life do you tend to have a negative dialogue about? How can you creatively speak about them to get a better feeling?

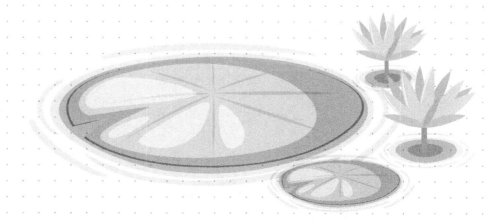

An older friend of mine named Theo recently told me a story of how the first thing she does when she looks at her reflection in the mirror every morning is making a silly face. That really resonated with me. I started looking for ways to take life less seriously and stop critiquing my own reflection. Our natural state is to feel good!

So let's start by minimizing the *can't* and *don't* in our dialogue and start expanding our vocabulary to create a new habit of speaking in a kinder, more gentle way to ourselves and others. Your body will reward you in return!

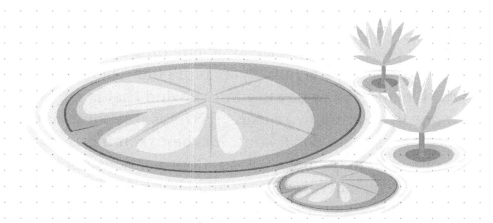

The Appreciation Challenge

Here is what my morning routine was for most of my adult life. I was jolted awake by my alarm going off at 5 a.m. This instantly made me grumpy because I felt like I never got enough sleep. Tired 24/7. My brain then switches to 'what day is it' and from there what needs to be accomplished in that day. Grumpily, I get out of bed and seek help in a cup of coffee. Ok, I'm starting to feel a bit more alive. I would grab a donut or toast (or some other unhealthy thing) and plunk down in front of the morning news. Then, it's up to get dressed and out the door. Go, go, go all day until I'm exhausted and crawl into bed by 9 p.m. Another day . . . gone.

Thank goodness that this is no longer my routine but does any of this resemble yours? I was not paying attention to the details. I was not setting my intent for the day. I was not being grateful for the act of just 'waking up' to live another day. What I really wanted was to wake up feeling good. I really wanted to find joy in my day. I really wanted to find inspiration, but I did not know where to start.

One day, I was given guidance by my Guardian Angel to count my blessings at sunrise and sunset. OK, this I could do. I could come up with one thing when I wake up and one thing when I go to sleep. I was not consistent at first and often-times forgot, but eventually, I got more in a habit and actually looked forward to the exercise! My list got longer and my blessings would just spur off each other until my list was endless and I could go on and on if I wanted to.

Now, I keep this exercise to just 5 minutes in the morning and again at night. Do you know what happens when you go to bed grateful and in a good mood? You wake up that same way! Often, I say how grateful I am for my bed. How grateful I am for having another day to have a physical experience here on Earth. In the morning, I will always throw in how grateful I am to have another day to make a difference in just one person's life.

I've been doing this exercise for a long time now and it has brought me to a point where I am living a genuinely inspired life. There is no such thing as a 'bad' day in my life now. Every day is a miracle and that is my perspective. Contrast comes into our lives for many reasons. Perhaps it is there to clarify what we truly want by seeing what we don't want. Maybe to remind us of how much good is in our life compared to the not-so-good. Contrast does not have to spiral us down into a bad day. Remember that life is all about how we react to it, and we create it with our thoughts.

Make a list of all the good things in your life. Once you start writing, it will start to flow and you will see just how much you have to be appreciative of. Then, I challenge you to take the 5 minutes before you get out of bed in the morning and 5 minutes before you fall asleep at night just to count your blessings.

Your Reality is not Your Neighbor's Reality

'Reality check'

'Lose touch with reality'

'Detached from reality'

'You don't live in reality'

We've all heard these idioms for reality but what exactly does 'reality' mean? Wikipedia defines reality as the sum or aggregate of all that is real or existent, as opposed to that which is only imaginary. Does that make it clearer? Not by much.

Let's use a scenario to help us understand. It's a beautiful sunny day and you go with your best friend into the city to do some shopping. As you're walking down the busy sidewalk together, you are enjoying the warm sun on your face, the birds chirping, and the smiles on the faces of people passing by. It's a great day. Your friend, walking beside you, is noticing the noise of the street, a car playing its radio too loud, and a person yelling into their phone. How is it that you and your friend are having such different experiences in the same place at the same time? Are you both experiencing the same reality?

The answer is simple. You are not. Each person *creates* their own reality by how they *think*. Read that again. Now this concept took me a while to wrap my head around too. After all, we are programmed to think that there is only ONE reality. But how can that be true? Think of the scenario above in which two people walking down the same street have very different experiences. The truth is that we are each living our *own* reality. We are creating it every single day with our thoughts. Now, it can be possible to find someone who thinks like you in which your realities may be quite similar. This would be our goal in finding a partner for sure.

Your reality is also made up of inclusion. In other words, what you choose to include in your life. If you choose to include all the negativity and bias of the news media, this becomes part of your reality. If you choose to spend time in nature and surrounded by happy people, this becomes part of your reality. If you wake up in the morning thinking that this is going to be a great day, your day will flow well. When your days flow well, your life flows well.

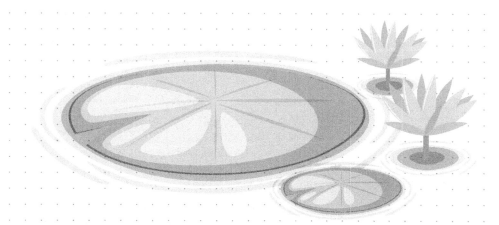

Do you see how you can take back your power? It's never too late to create the reality you want. You can start today by swapping out more positive thoughts for the negative ones. You can start today by including into your life only those things that make you happy.

And the next time someone says to you that 'you don't live in reality', you are going to smile and take that as a compliment because you now know that you don't have to accept someone else's version of reality as your own. You are creating your own life experience, one thought at a time.

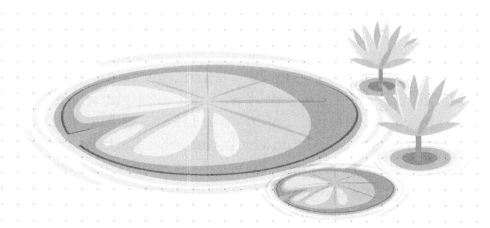

Attitude of Gratitude

Renowned gratitude expert Robert Emmons argues that gratitude has two main parts. *"First, it's an affirmation of goodness. We affirm that there are good things in the world, gifts and benefits we've received."* He explains the second part of gratitude as more social. *"We recognize that the sources of this goodness are outside of ourselves... We acknowledge that other people—or even higher powers... gave us many gifts, big and small, to help us achieve the goodness in our lives."* Emmons also writes, *"I see it as a relationship-strengthening emotion because it requires us to see how we've been supported and affirmed by other people."*

'An affirmation of goodness'. The description of gratitude brings just as much warmth to me as the word itself. If you were to meditate on that word, gratitude, for a few minutes, what would be the first thing that comes to your mind? Did it surprise you or is it something you expected? When I think about gratitude, I think about a lot of things, but predominantly people. I think about those people in my life that played a major role in my personal development.

I think about being that extremely shy young adult compared to the empowered, outgoing woman I am now. I will forever feel deep gratitude for all the patience that was graciously given to me in teaching me how to be the immensely independent person of today. There are few people in this world who truly invest in another person and their success. We need more of those people; the ones who are willing to share their never-ending patience and knowledge.

We also need our cheerleaders, our fans, our tribe, to support us in any and every inspired idea we come up with. These people will always be in our corner and I'm so grateful that I can easily list the names of mine. They come from my relationships, my friends and my family.

Gratitude for a place that is home. A place of my own that calls to me when I am away. A place that wraps me in serenity the moment I walk through the door. A place that keeps me safe and warm. My home had no well, no insulation, and only an old wood stove that was not air tight when I moved in almost 10 years ago. It was a summer camp on a lake that had my name on the deed so when my life turned upside down, it was all I had. In that first year of trying to live in that camp, I seriously doubted my sanity on several occasions. I had to race home every night after work to start a fire in the woodstove because it would be completely out and the camp bordering on freezing.

I didn't always win the race. A few times the pipes froze. I would stand with my back to the woodstove trying to stay warm and watch my breath come out in puffs in the cold air in front of me. My alarm was set to wake me up every 2 hours at night because if I didn't keep putting wood in the stove, it would go out. In a cold Maine winter, that's something you did not want to happen. After that first year, I would trade out my woodstove for a small furnace and started sleeping through the night. I am so grateful for that furnace. Electricity had become a gift and was never to be taken for granted. I was able to borrow a friend's gas generator and learned how to hook it up to at least keep my furnace going.

One night in November I came home to no electricity and started going through the motions of getting the generator set up. The first pull on the crank left the handle in my hand and the rest of the cord wrapped up inside the generator. At that moment, I had never felt so defeated. I got back in my truck where it was warm and I cried. What I was trying to do was absolutely impossible for a woman to handle all by herself and I fell into that mindset miserably. Years later, I have a big generator that automatically comes on and runs my entire camp when the power goes out. I am so grateful when I hear that generator humming.

There are things that we are thankful for and things that we are grateful for. I have made sure to tell that person how grateful I am in gifting me my fierce independence. I have made sure to tell my camp often of how thankful I am that not only did I not give up on it, but it did not give up on me.

Grateful comes deep, straight from the heart. The act of being grateful means that something or someone has deeply touched your life. We need to remind ourselves each day of that which makes us grateful.

Change the Channel

Energy is a vibration. It is a frequency. Our bodies tune into it like when you tune your car radio into a particular station. Everything around us is made up of energy and our bodies are experts in interpretation. You don't have to consciously *do* anything. However, you will *know* what frequency you just tuned into by the way your body is responding.

Here you are driving along in your car and a song comes on with a good uplifting beat and your finger starts tapping the steering wheel. Your body is interpreting the good vibration coming from the music and is responding. You may even start singing along. The positive energy is well received by your body. You have now arrived at home just in time to turn on the evening news. You are listening to the news stories as you prepare for dinner. The news announcer is telling about a tragic outcome that happened in a local town, followed by another story of poverty in some foreign land, and it goes on and on, one negative story after another.

Remember that amazing feeling you had back in your car? The big smile you had on your face as you walked into your house? Now, you find yourself feeling a little bit short-tempered. So what happened here? What happened to all that joy you had going when you got home? As your evening progressed, your body was sending you subtle little nudges, small signs that something you don't really want is coming. Because you weren't paying attention, you missed the warning signs and now here you are in a total opposite feeling space than where you were.

I learned this lesson first hand a few years ago. Waking up in my usual good mood, I went about my morning fixing my breakfast, watching the morning news, and then leaving it on while I finished getting ready. My dog was just being his normal, overly attentive to his human, self that morning but as I went through the motions of my daily routine I was getting more and more frustrated with him always being in my way. It got to the point where I actually yelled at him.

 That was my wake up call, literally. All of a sudden I was aware that I was in a totally different space emotionally than when I woke up. That's when I heard it. The tv just in the other room was still sending its negative energy out into my camp with one news story after another. Instantly, I went to the living room and turned it off, feeling instant relief. I came to the realization that my body was still picking up the vibration from those news stories and was affecting me in a negative way.

This became a turning point in my life. It was then that I started turning off the news when a negative story would come on. My awareness of the vibrations around me started heightening to the point where I made a New Year Resolution to no longer watch the news. I cared so much about the way I felt that I only wanted to feel *good*. I now walk away from negativity in any form and yes, that includes people. No longer do I hold space for negativity.

When you want to start making changes in your life to allow more positive and less negative, you need to start paying attention to how your body is interpreting the energy around it.

If you are not happy with the signal you are getting, remember you always have the option to Change the Channel!

17 Seconds

How do you feel about today? Was it a good day or did you feel like you were on an emotional rollercoaster? I think we all intend to start each day with good expectations. So what exactly goes wrong? We need to aspire to take control of our thoughts. Our thoughts are so powerful that they can determine our days, our months, our years, and ultimately our life.

A really good concept is the thought guidance of 17 Seconds introduced by Abraham Hicks. The idea is that if you can recognize and redirect from a non-beneficial thought within 17 seconds that you will be able to keep yourself from spiraling down a deconstructive path of negativity. This is how our mind builds from thought to thought.

For instance, let's take a look in the mirror and you say to yourself 'I don't like how that extra 20 pounds looks on me'. 'It's all that bad food I eat'. 'My life would be so much better if I didn't have that extra 20 pounds'. 'Why can't I lose it?' 'My co-worker always looks so thin, why can't I be like her'. 'I'll never be thin so why do I even try'. 'I really hate my body'.

Once you hold a negative thought or belief long enough, another one like it will follow. Then, another and another until now you feel 10 times worse than when you started and you find yourself in a bad mood. So let's take control. It will take practice because after all, we are reprogramming how you process your thoughts. The next time you look in the mirror and start to criticize yourself, stop, implement the 17 Second Rule and redirect. 'I don't like how that extra 20 pounds looks on me'. 'But I really do have a beautiful smile'. 'It makes me feel good when people comment on it'.

You have just redirected your thoughts to something that makes you feel good which was followed by the thought of how you get compliments. You successfully stopped yourself from going down that rabbit hole which would have resulted in a bad mood, low self-esteem and possibly even anxiety surrounding your weight. There is never any benefit gained from holding yourself in a negative thought pattern and if held long enough, that thought state will start affecting your physical health.

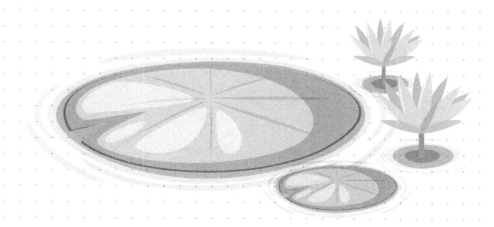

However, holding in a positive thought pattern creates a sense of peace and happiness. You will find that you no longer ride that emotional rollercoaster. You will start having a lot more good days with some really fantastic days sprinkled in there. All controlled by YOU.

Start right now using the 17 Second Rule. Have some thoughts that are your backup for when you find yourself entertaining a non-beneficial thought so that you can easily redirect your thinking. Any easily-accessible positive thought will work, things such as puppies playing, the sound of your child laughing, whatever instantly puts a smile on your face, that's what I want you to make a list of and have ready.

Your days will become happier as your thoughts become happier.

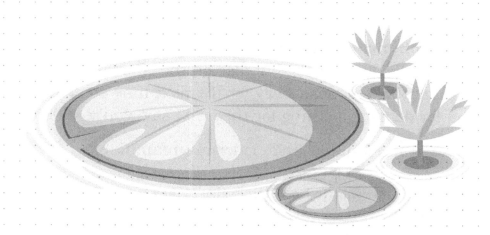

Get Comfortable with Praise

Christopher Littlefield, the founder of AcknowledgementWorks, interviewed over three hundred people over the course of a year while riding the subway in Boston. His research found that although the number one thing people associate with being recognized is a feeling of being valued (88%), nearly 70% also associate recognition with embarrassment or discomfort. Most of us can't take a compliment and often don't even realize it! According to Littlefield, "Recognition is often more about the giver than the receiver." So what does that actually mean?

Have you ever told someone, 'that's a beautiful sweater' only to have them say, 'oh this old thing?' Why is it so hard for us to believe that our sweater can be so beautiful that someone would go out of their way to compliment us on it? Actually responding with a 'thank you' feels uncomfortable, most likely stemming back from our upbringing. We are often encouraged to discard and deflect recognition as a way to 'stay humble'.

We aren't realizing that a compliment is actually a gift that we are receiving from another person. If you were gifted a hideous plaid shirt by your in-laws at Christmas, you would not throw it back in their faces. You would graciously tell them, thank you. The same grace applies to being given the gift of compliments.

Being 100% guilty of this myself, I have been working on reprogramming my negative automatic response to praise. I have no issue in giving the gift of praise to others (which in itself is an accomplishment from a life lived behind the curtain of shyness) and now I've learned to receive the gift as well.

Since becoming aware of this phenomenon, I take note of how people respond to my compliments. You'll find that only a small percentage are actually comfortable saying 'thank you' or 'you're welcome' back to you.

Let's work not only on the effort to compliment our bosses, employees, co-workers, family, and friends, but also on the effort in ourselves to receive praise openly. Tuck this response away for the next time someone walks up to you to thank you for doing something for them . . . say 'you're welcome'.

Make praise familiar and criticism unfamiliar.

* Adapted from What To Do When Praise Makes You Uncomfortable by Mark Goulston, Harvard Business Review, December 2013.

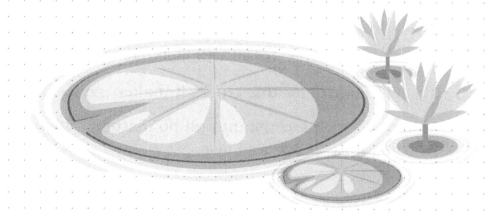

Happiness Habits

As I've described, my days are a flow of mindful moments where I intentionally notice and amplify appreciation. Here's how a typical day might flow.

1. Count my blessings before I get out of bed, even if it's just to say how thankful I am for this amazing bed. Please let me make a difference in one person's life today.

2. Meditate on happy thoughts and my inspirations and eliminate the morning news.

3. Put on my playlist of happy songs with high vibrations.

4. Start my day, whether it's a work day or day off, by maintaining positive thinking and using the 17 Second Rule on anything non-beneficial that slips into my mind.

5. Give the gift of a compliment as often as I can and receive the gift of a compliment with grace and a heartfelt response.

6. Sitting here in traffic gives me the opportunity to admire how beautiful the sky is today.

7. Clearly, this angry person in front of me in line must be having a bad day. I wonder what his journey is like. I'm going to smile at him.

8. These shoes are so comfy.

9. My dog is always so happy to see me when I get home. I'm going to take him for a walk tonight.

10. Another panhandler . . . is this part of the lesson he came here to learn in life or did he get off track? I wish him well.

11. I wonder what the sunset will look like tonight.

12. I'm so thankful for this truck. It makes me feel so safe.

13. Home . . . such a constant pull no matter how far I go. I'm glad it is so full of tranquility, peace and love.

14. As I'm preparing my dinner, I'm thinking about how I make such healthy choices now and my body is clearly thanking me for it in how I feel and in maintaining a healthy weight.

15. Time for a few minutes in front of some funny sitcoms that make me laugh out loud and keep my good vibes going.

16. Which book should I read tonight that will give me some positive insight into myself so I can be an even better person tomorrow than I am today?

17. It's Bedtime and I'm so thankful for this amazing bed and the restful night of sleep it will give me. Count my blessings.

Money Really Does Grow on Trees

What if I told you that your thoughts are so powerful that you ARE what you THINK?

I AM . . . always broke.

I AM . . . never going to be able to afford that new car.

I AM . . . always behind in paying my bills.

Do you get the picture yet? Here is where some MAJOR re-programming needs to happen. We have been programmed to think that we can only acquire things if we work hard. We must sacrifice to get ahead. We must earn our money because it does not come freely.

How does it FEEL when you say, I AM... abundant? That feels much easier on your nervous system. Your brain may not be able to process that phrase yet but we are going to show it how to. To this day, I am still working on undoing all the non-beneficial beliefs that were instilled upon me. I shared in an earlier lesson that I stopped balancing my checkbook years ago. By micro-managing every penny, I was creating excess stress on my body by needing to make sure every purchase and deposit was accounted for.

The most unbelievable freedom comes when you 'let go' of something that you have a stranglehold on. Now, we do need to be good stewards of our money and have a basic knowledge of how much comes in compared to how much goes out. That is about as much depth as I go with it, however.

Esther and Jerry Hicks have a book called 'Money and the Law of Attraction'. They offer many simple exercises of reprogramming your thoughts surrounding money. I highly recommend starting to play around with your thoughts on money. The majority of our thoughts surrounding money and wealth tend to be negative due to the beliefs that were passed down to us from others. That does not mean that those beliefs are TRUE. Abraham Hicks tells us 'a belief is only a thought that you keep thinking'.

One of the exercises is to write yourself a check. So I got out my checkbook and wrote myself a check for $50,000 and signed it from the 'Universe'. That was three years ago. That was the amount of money I thought I needed to finish remodeling my camp into a lake house. Did I ever receive the lump sum of $50,000? No, I did not.

However, I did start receiving the *value* of the $50,000 in the form of a job promotion, offers to teach on the side, back pay, sale of family property, as well as free services from people offering to help me work on my camp, and countless other methods. Even today, I am continuing to receive value.

When an unexpected bill comes in, my thought process goes to my catchphrase . . . "There is always an abundance of money".

I AM . . . abundant.

I AM . . . a money magnet.

I AM . . . worthy of having money.

There is an abundance of EVERYTHING in the universe. There is no LACK. If you are feeling lack in any area of your life, it is because you think there is lack and are holding yourself in that thought pattern, you and only you. No one else can create lack for you just as no one can create abundance for you.

Here is the key. Be specific in what you are asking for, but do not be specific in the form in which you want to receive it. Start small, such as asking for $20 to buy that pair of shoes you want and remain 'open' to all the possible ways that it will come to you. Don't forget, someone can simply *give you* that particular pair of shoes and the $20 is completely bypassed. Expect a miracle and you will receive a miracle.

For me, money does grow on trees. When I want something, I know that the money will be in my bank account when it's time for me to need it or I expect the universe to use one of its miraculous ways to bring it into my life.

Stay in Your Lane

Ever find yourself driving down the road on a bright sunny day, your favorite channel on the radio is pushing out good vibes filling your vehicle, you are totally immersed in this carefree feeling and then, all of a sudden, one of your tires hits the rumble strip in the center of the road? You are snapped back into the moment, song forgotten, carefree feeling left back there somewhere on the road behind you.

So what just happened?

When we are tuned into our good feeling emotions, life flows really well. We find our job is less stressful, our family life is more harmonious, and we can find more inspiration in even the little things in life such as watching a bee gathering nectar from a flower. The emotional rollercoaster that used to be our 'normal' is a distant memory. We have learned to use our emotional guidance system to recognize what feels good and we only move toward those things.

As we create more and more awareness of how we feel, we will be able to react faster when a non-beneficial thought or feeling comes into our lane. As soon as one of our tires starts to cross that rumble strip, all the bells and whistles in your body will start going off declaring warning, warning! You do NOT want to continue down this path! This is not where you want to be! Go back! Go back! GO BACK!

That rumble strip is there for a reason . . . so you don't hit the tree. Hitting a tree is not pretty, especially at a high rate of speed. I know. I've been there. Recently I put myself in a situation where I felt the rumble strip. I heard the warning bells. My body was reacting accordingly with disappointment, anger, and frustration.

Still, I pursued this 'thing' I thought I wanted in my life. Even at the level of awareness that I hold myself at today with feeling good, sometimes I tell myself that I know better than my emotions. This never ends well for me.

Maybe it's just human nature to force things; to pursue things that are not good for us. I'm not an expert on human behavior but I am turning out to be quite an expert on *me*. In pursuit of this 'thing', the Universe intervened with roadblock after roadblock. I drove right through them. Thank goodness that finally my emotional guidance system overrode my mind and I stopped dead in the road at the THIRD roadblock. I regained control of my vehicle and steered determinedly back into my lane with a renewed purpose. I will STAY IN MY LANE in all the pursuits in my life. I will stay in the Flow Lane.

If what you want is not coming easily to you, then you are going about it all wrong. Slightly pull off to the side of the road and evaluate your journey. Put everything back in perspective, and then put that vehicle back in Drive.

You've got this, my friends. The momentum of your life is totally up to you. Fast or slow, as long as you stay in alignment with who you truly are, then good feeling emotions will continue to flow and you can drive that car 60 MPH down that highway or 10 MPH and life will be a constant joy.

Living life on a plateau of happiness is your reality now. Savor it. Immerse yourself in it.

You came here for the experience, make it a good one.

Additional Reading Resources

The Universe Has Your Back by Gabrielle Bernstein

Super Attractor by Gabrielle Bernstein

The Secret by Rhonda Byrne

The Law of Attraction by Esther and Jerry Hicks

The Astonishing Power of Emotions by Esther and Jerry Hicks

How to be Your Own Genie by Radleigh Valentine

Your Flow Lane Journey

To continue flowing with Lynn:

Feel free to reach out by email to lynn.reikiwellness@gmail.com with any questions or comments on the material presented in this workbook.

You may also follow Wine and Spirits Book Club, a Facebook page dedicated to inspirational books with a spiritual twist. Lynn introduces a new book every few months. Members may opt to read the books and they are encouraged to comment if they feel inspired.

In addition, Morning Coffee Meditation is a Facebook page where Lynn hand-selects a positive inspirational quote each morning. Members are free to share and comment on any quote that resonates with them.

The Unbelievable Freedom Habit Guide Series

If you enjoyed this book and would like to continue your
Unbelievable Freedom journey, there are other titles to collect!

Fasting Feasting Freedom: A 33 Day Habit Creation Guide by Kim Smith

Poster Girl Habits: Creating an Intentional Contentment Practice by Kim Smith

A Superhero You: Activate Your Unstoppable Powers by Barbara Anne Cookson

Embracing Next: An Empty Nest Enjoyment Guide by Kim Smith

And coming soon...

Script Your Life: A Guide to Lasting Change Creation by Tam Veilleux

Information about all of these workbook-style Habit Guides
can be found at www.unbelievablefreedom.com,
along with links to their Amazon listings.

Believe in Unbelievable Freedom

Enjoy Your Life!

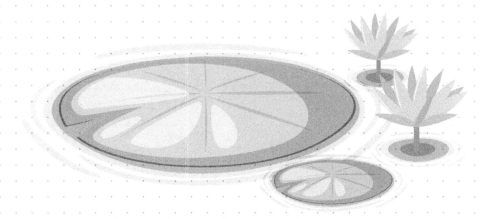

Made in the USA
Coppell, TX
07 February 2021

49900996R00039